DSMC Chanting Book

ISBN:-13 978-1499705065, ISBN-10 1499705069

Dhamma Sukha Meditation Center

8218 County Road 204

Annapolis, MO 63620

U.S.A.

Phone: +1 (573) 546-1214

[URL: www.dhammasukha.org]

Email: info@dhammasukha.org

DSMC Chanting Book

Overseen by Bhante Vimalaraṃsi

Compiled by Bhante Kusala

Formatted by Sister Khema

Printed by David Johnson

TABLE OF CONTENTS

	Page
1. ***Namakkāraṃ*** (Homage to the *Buddha*)	8
2. ***Tisaraṇa*** (Taking the Three Refuges)	9
3. ***Aṭṭha sikkhā*** (Eight Precepts)	10
4. ***Buddha-guṇa-vandanā***	
(Worshipping the virtues of the *Buddha*)	12
5. ***Dhamma-guṇa-vandanā***	
(Worshipping the virtues of the *Dhamma*)	13
6. ***Saṅgha-guṇa-vandanā***	
(Worshipping the virtues of the *Saṅgha*)	14
7. ***Patthanā*** (Wish)	15
8. ***Paṭicca samuppāda*** (Dependent Co-Origination)	16
9. ***Ovāda pātimokkha gāthā***	
(Admonition on monastic code)	19
10. ***Āmisa pūjā*** (Material Offerings)	20
a. The main objects of veneration	
b. Lights	
c. Incense	
d. Water	
e. Flowers	
11. ***Ākaṅkhā*** (Aspiration)	22
12. ***Paṭipatti pūjā*** (Offering the Practice)	22
13. ***Khamā yācanā*** (Asking for forgiveness)	23
14. ***Devārādhanā*** (Invitation to the *Devas*)	24

Page

15. ***Mahā maṅgala suttaṃ***
(The Discourse on Great Blessings) 25

16. ***Ratana suttaṃ*** (The Discourse on the Gems) 29

17. ***Karaṇīya-metta suttaṃ***
(The Discourse on how *Mettā* should be practiced). 37

18. Khandha parittaṃ
(The Safeguard of the Constituent Groups) 40

19. ***Puññānumodanā*** (Transferring Merits) 41

20. ***Āsīvāda*** (Blessings) 42

21. A Guide to Pronunciation of Pali 43

1. NAMAKKĀRAṂ
HOMAGE TO THE BUDDHA

Namo tassa,
Homage to him,

Bhagavato,
the Blessed One,

Arahato,
the Worthy One,

Sammā-sambuddhassa.
the Fully Awakened One.

Namo tassa,
Homage to him,

Bhagavato,
the Blessed One,

Arahato,
the Worthy One,

Sammā-sambuddhassa.
the Fully Awakened One.

Namo tassa,
Homage to him

Bhagavato,
the Blessed One,

Arahato,
the Worthy One,

Sammā-sambuddhassa.
the Fully Awakened One.

2. TISARAṆA
TAKING THE THREE REFUGES

Buddhaṃ saraṇaṃ gacchāmi
I take refuge in the Buddha

Dhammaṃ saraṇaṃ gacchāmi
I take refuge in the Dhamma

Saṅghaṃ saraṇaṃ gacchāmi
I take refuge in the Saṅgha

Dutiyampi buddhaṃ saraṇaṃ gacchāmi
For the second time, I take refuge in the Buddha

Dutiyampi dhammaṃ saraṇaṃ gacchāmi
For the second time, I take refuge in the Dhamma

Dutiyampi saṅghaṃ saraṇaṃ gacchāmi
For the second time, I take refuge in the Saṅgha

Tatiyampi buddhaṃ saraṇaṃ gacchāmi
For the third time, I take refuge in the Buddha

Tatiyampi dhammaṃ saraṇaṃ gacchāmi
For the third time, I take refuge in the Dhamma

Tatiyampi saṅghaṃ saraṇaṃ gacchāmi
For the third time, I take refuge in the Saṅgha

3. AṬṬHA SIKKHĀ
EIGHT PRECEPTS

1. ***Pāṇāti-pātā veramaṇī sikkhā-padaṃ samādiyāmi.***
   I undertake the training precept to abstain from killing or harming living beings on purpose.

2. ***Adinnā-dānā veramaṇī sikkhā-padaṃ samādiyāmi.***
   I undertake the training precept to abstain from taking what is not given.

3. ***Abrahma-cariyā veramaṇī-sikkhā-padaṃ samādiyāmi.***
   I undertake the training precept to abstain from all sexual activity.

4. ***Musāvādā veramaṇī sikkhā-padaṃ samādiyāmi.***
   I undertake the training precept to abstain from telling lies, harsh speech, slander, and gossip
   .

5. ***Surā meraya-majja-pamā-daṭṭhānā veramaṇī sikkhā-padaṃ samādiyāmi.***
   I undertake the training precept to abstain from taking any kind of intoxicants.

6. ***Vikāla-bhojanā veramaṇī sikkhā-padaṃ samādiyāmi.***
   I undertake the training precept to abstain from taking solid food after the noon day meal (from 12:00 noon until dawn).

7. ***Nacca'-gīta, vādita, visūka-dassana, mālā, gandha, vilepana, dhāraṇa, maṇḍana, vibhūsa-naṭṭhānā veramaṇī sikkhā-padaṃ samādiyāmi.***
   I undertake the training precept to abstain from dancing, singing, music, and any unwholesome entertainment show, the use of flowers, garlands, perfumes, unguents and things that tend to beautify and adorn a person.

8. ***Mettā-saha-gatena cetasā sabba-pāṇa bhūta hitānu-kampī viharāmīti sikkhā padaṃ samādiyāmi.***
   I undertake the training precept to dwell with my mind pervading loving-kindness toward myself and all beings as often as possible in life.

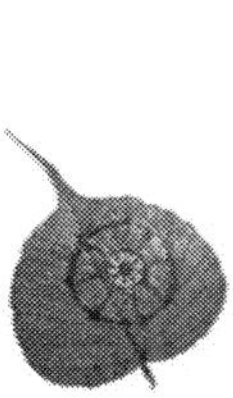

4. BUDDHA-GUṆA-VANDANĀ
WORSHIPPING THE VIRTUES OF THE BUDDHA

Iti pi so,
Such is he,

Bhagavā,
the Blessed One,

Arahaṃ,
the Worthy One,

Sammā-sambuddho,
the Fully Awakened One.

vijjā-caraṇa-sampanno,
the one endowed with understanding and good conduct,

Sugato,
the Fortunate One,

Lokavidū,
the one who understands the worlds,

Anuttaro, purisa-damma-sārathī,
the unsurpassed guide for those people who need taming,

Satthā deva-manussānaṃ,
the Teacher of gods and men,

Buddho,
the Buddha,

Bhagavā ti.
the Blessed One.

5. DHAMMA-GUṆA-VANDANĀ
WORSHIPPING THE VIRTUES OF THE DHAMMA

Svākkhāto bhagavatā dhammo,
The Dhamma has been well-proclaimed by the Blessed One,

sandiṭṭhiko,
it is visable,

akāliko,
immediately effective,

ehi-passiko,
inviting inspection,

opanayiko,
onward leading,

paccattaṃ vedi-tabbo viññūhī ti.
and can be understood by the wise for themselves.

6. SAṄGHA-GUṆA-VANDANĀ
WORSHIPPING THE VIRTUES OF THE SAṄGHA

Supaṭipanno bhagavato, sāvaka-saṅgho,
The Blessed One's Saṅgha of disciples are good in their practice,

uju-paṭipanno bhagavato, sāvaka-saṅgho,
the Blessed One's Saṅgha of disciples are straight in their practice,

ñāya-paṭipanno bhagavato, sāvaka-saṅgho,
the Blessed One's Saṅgha of disciples are systematic in their practice,

sāmīci-paṭipanno bhagavato, sāvaka-saṅgho,
the Blessed One's Saṅgha of disciples are correct in their practice,

yadidaṃ cattāri purisa-yugāni, aṭṭha purisa-puggalā,
that is to say, the four pairs of persons, the eight individual persons,

esa bhagavato, sāvaka-saṅgho,
this is the Blessed One's Saṅgha of disciples,

āhuneyyo, pāhuneyyo, dakkhiṇeyyo, añjali-karanīyo,
they are worthy of offerings, of hospitality, of gifts, and of reverential salutation,

anuttaraṃ puññakkhettaṃ, lokassā ti.
they are an unsurpassed field of merit for the world.

7. PATTHANĀ
WISH

Icceva-maccanta namassaneyyaṃ,
In this way, I can revere the three gems without end,

namassamāno ratanattayaṃ yaṃ,
and while revering them,

puññā-bhi-sandhaṃ vipulaṃ alatthaṃ,
I have received an abundant overflow of merit,

tassā-nubhāvena hatantarāyo!
by that power may (any) obstacle be destroyed!

8. PAṬICCA SAṂ-UPPĀDA
DEPENDENT CO-ORIGINATION

ANULOMAṂ - THE ORDER OF ARISING

Avijjā paccayā, saṅkhārā.
Dependent on ignorance, formations arise.
Saṅkhāra paccayā, viññāṇaṃ.
Dependent on formations, consciousness arises.
Viññāṇa paccayā, nāma rūpaṃ.
Dependent on consciousness, mentality/materiality arise.
Nāma rūpa paccayā, saḷāyatanaṃ.
Dependent on mentality/materiality, the six-fold base arises.
Saḷāyatana paccayā, phasso.
Dependent on the six-fold base, contact arises.
Phassa paccayā, vedanā.
Dependent on contact, feeling arises.
Vedanā paccayā, taṇhā.
Dependent on feeling, craving arises.
Taṇhā paccayā, upādānaṃ.
Dependent on craving, clinging arises.
Upādāna paccayā, bhavo.
Dependent on clinging, becoming arises.
Bhava paccayā, jāti.
Dependent on becoming, birth arises.

Jāti paccayā, jarā maraṇaṃ, soka parideva, dukkha domanass'upāyāsā sambhavanti.
Dependent on birth, aging and death,
sorrow, lamentation, pain, grief, and despair (arise).
Evametassa kevalassa dukkha-kkhandhassa samudayo hoti.
Thus, there is the arising of this whole mass of suffering.

PAṬILOMAṂ - THE ORDER OF CESSATION

Avijjāya tve'va asesa virāga nirodhā, saṅkhāra nirodho.
Through the entire cessation of this ignorance, volitional formations cease.
Saṅkhāra nirodhā, viññāṇa nirodho.
Through the cessation of volitional formations, consciousness ceases.
Viññāṇa nirodhā, nāma rūpa nirodho.
Through the cessation of consciousness, mentality and materiality cease.
Nāma rūpa nirodhā, saḷāyatana nirodho.
Through the cessation of mentality and materiality, the six-fold base ceases.
Saḷāyatana nirodhā, phassa nirodho.
Through the cessation of the sixfold base, contact ceases.
Phassa nirodhā, vedanā nirodho.
Through the cessation of feeling, craving ceases.
Vedanā nirodhā, taṇhā nirodho.
Through the cessation of contact, feeling ceases.
Taṇhā nirodhā, upādāna nirodho.
Through the cessation of craving, clinging ceases.

Upādāna nirodhā, bhava nirodho.
Through the cessation of clinging, becoming ceases.
Bhava nirodhā, jāti nirodho.
Through the cessation of becoming, birth ceases.
Jāti nirodhā, jarā-maraṇaṃ soka parideva dukkha domanass'upāyāsā nirujjhanti
Through the cessation of birth, aging and death , sorrow, lamentation, pain, grief, and despair cease.
Evametassa kevalassa dukkha-kkhandhassa nirodho hotī'ti
Thus, there is the cessation of this whole mass of suffering.

9. OVĀDA-PĀTIMOKKHA GĀTHĀ
ADMONITION ON MONASTIC CODE

Khantī paramaṃ tapo tītikkhā
Patient forbearance is the foremost austerity.
Nibbānaṃ paramaṃ vadanti buddhā,
Nibbāna is foremost: that's what the Buddhas say.
Na hi pabbajito parūpa-ghātī
He is not a monk who injures another;
Samaṇo hoti paraṃ viheṭhayanto
nor a contemplative, he who mistreats another.
Sabba-pāpassa akaraṇaṃ,
The non-doing of any evil,
Kusalassa upasampadā,
The performance of what's skillful,
Sacitta-pariyo-dapanaṃ:
The cleansing of one's own mind:
Etaṃ buddhāna-sāsanaṃ.
This is the Buddhas' teaching.
Anūpa-vādo anūpa-ghāto
Not disparaging, not injuring,
Pātimokkhe ca saṃvaro
Restraint in line with the monastic code,
Mattaññutā ca bhattasmiṃ
Moderation in food,
Pantañca sayanāsanaṃ.
Dwelling in seclusion,
Adhicitte ca āyogo:
Commitment to the heightened mind:
Etaṃ buddhāna-sāsananti.
This is the admonition of the Buddhas'

10. AMISA-PŪJĀ - MATERIAL OFFERINGS

(Only chant verses for what you are offering)

a. THE MAIN OBJECTS OF VENERATION

Vandāmi cetiyaṃ sabbaṃ, sabba-ṭhānesu patiṭṭhitaṃ,
I worship all the *cetiyas*, in all of the places that they stand,
sārīrika-dhātu mahā bodhiṃ, buddha-rūpaṃ sakalaṃ sadā!
the bodily relics, the great bodhi tree, and all the Buddha images forever!

b. LIGHTS

Ghana-sārappa-dittena, dīpena tama-dhaṃsinā,
With a lamp that burns intensely, destroying the darkness,
tiloka-dīpaṃ sambuddhaṃ, pūjayāmi tamonudaṃ.
I worship the Sambuddha, the light of the three worlds, the darkness-dispeller.

c. INCENSE

Sugandhi-kāya-vadanaṃ, ananta-guṇa-gandhinā,
With this fragrance and perfume, I worship the Tathāgata,
Sugandhinā-haṃ gandhena, pūjayāmi tathāgataṃ.
who is fragrant in body and speech, and has endless virtues.

d. WATER

Sugandhaṃ sītalaṃ kappaṃ, pasanna-madhuraṃ subhaṃ,
Please accept this fragrant, cool, clear, sweet, and pleasant drink
pānīya-metaṃ bhagavā, patigaṇhātu-muttama!
that has been prepared, O Bhagavā, the One supreme!

e. FLOWERS

Vaṇṇa-gandha-guṇo-petaṃ, etaṃ kusuma-santatiṃ,
With these long lasting flowers, endowed with the qualities of beauty and fragrance,
pūjayāmi munindassa, sirīpāda-saroruhe.
I worship the glorious lotus feet of the lord of Sages.
***Pūjemi Buddhaṃ kusamena-nena, puññena-metena labhāmi* mokkhaṃ.**
I worship the Awakened One with these flowers, may I gain release with this merit.
Pupphaṃ milāyāti yathā idaṃ me, kāyo tathā yāti vināsa-bhāvaṃ.
Just as a flower withers and fades away, so too this my body will go to destruction.

11. ĀKAṄKHĀ

ASPIRATION

Imāya buddha-pūjāya, katāya suddha-cetasā,
By this worship of the Buddha, performed with a pure mind,

ciraṃ tiṭṭhatu saddhammo, loko hotu sukhī sadā!
may the true dhamma last a long time, and may the world be happy!

12. PAṬIPATTI PŪJĀ

OFFERING THE PRACTICE

Imāya dhammānu-dhamma paṭipattiyā, buddhaṃ pūjemi.
By this practise of dhamma, in accord with the dhamma,
I worship the Buddha.

Imāya dhammānu-dhamma paṭipattiyā, dhammaṃ pūjemi.
By this practise of dhamma, in accord with the dhamma,
I venerate the Dhamma.

Imāya dhammānu-dhamma paṭipattiyā, saṅghaṃ pūjemi.
By this practise of *dhamma*, in accord with the *dhamma*,
I venerate the Saṅgha.

13. KHAMĀ YĀCANĀ
ASKING FOR FORGIVENESS

Kāyena vācā cittena,
By body, speech or mind,

pamādena mayā kataṃ,
if, due to negligence, I have done some wrong,

accayaṃ khama me Bhante
forgive me of that offence, O Bhante,

bhūri-pañña tathāgata.
Perfect One of vast wisdom.

14. DEVĀRĀDHANĀ
THE INVITATION TO THE DEVAS

(Chanted by One Person)
Samantā cakka-vāḷesu, atrā-gacchantu devatā
May the gods from all over the universe assemble here

saddhammaṃ muni rājassa, suṇantu sagga-mokkha-daṃ:
and listen to the King of the Sage's true Dhamma that gives the path to heaven and release:

Dhammassavaṇa-kālo, ayaṃ bhadantā!
Venerable Ones, this is the time for hearing the dhamma!

Dhammassavaṇa-kālo, ayaṃ bhadantā!
Venerable Ones, this is the time for hearing the dhamma!

Paritta-dhammassavaṇa-kālo ayaṃ bhadantā!
Venerable Ones, this is the time for hearing the safeguard recitals!

15. MAHĀ MAṄGALA SUTTAṂ
DISCOURSE ON THE GREAT BLESSINGS.

Evaṃ me sutaṃ, ekaṃ samayaṃ bhagavā, Sāvatthiyaṃ viharati jetavane anātha-piṇḍikassa ārāme.

Thus I have heard, at one time, the Blessed One was dwelling near Sāvatthi at Anāthapiṇḍika's *ārāma* in Jeta's Wood.

Atha kho aññatarā devatā, abhikkantāya rattiyā,

Then a certain god, towards the end of the night,

abhikkanta-vaṇṇā, kevala-kappaṃ Jetavanaṃ obhāsetvā,

having lit up the whole of Jeta's Wood with his surpassing beauty,

yena bhagavā, tenupasaṅkami,

approached where the Blessed One was,

upasaṅkamitvā, Bhagavantaṃ abhivādetvā, ekamantaṃ aṭṭhāsi.

and after approaching, and worshipping the Blessed One, he stood on one side.

Ekamantaṃ ṭhitā kho sā devatā, bhagavantaṃ gāthāya ajjhabhāsi:

While standing on one side that god addressed the Blessed One with a verse:

"Bahū devā manussā ca, maṅgalāni acintayuṃ

"Many are the gods and the men who have thought about the blessings

ākaṅkha-mānā sotthānaṃ: brūhi maṅgala-muttamaṃ."

hoping for safety: now please say what is the supreme blessing."

"Asevanā ca bālānaṃ, paṇḍitānañ ca sevanā,
"Not associating with fools, but associating with the wise,
pūjā ca pūja-nīyānaṃ: etaṃ maṅgala-muttamaṃ.
honouring those worthy of honour: this is the supreme blessing.
Patirūpa-desa-vāso ca, pubbe ca kata-puññatā,
Living in a suitable place, formerly having done good deeds,
atta-sammā-paṇidhi ca: etaṃ maṅgala-muttamaṃ.
aspiring in a right way oneself: this is the supreme blessing.

Bāhu-saccañ-ca sippañ-ca, vinayo ca susikkhito,
Having great learning and craft, and being disciplined and well trained,
subhāsitā ca yā vācā: etaṃ maṅgala-muttamaṃ.
and if the words are well spoken: this is the supreme blessing.
Mātā-pitu-upaṭṭhānaṃ, putta-dārassa saṅgaho,
Attendance on one's mother and father, looking after one's wife and children,
anākulā ca kammantā: etaṃ maṅgala-muttamaṃ.
with works that are not agitating: this is the supreme blessing.

Dānañ-ca dhamma-cariyā ca, ñātakānañ-ca saṅgaho,
Giving, and living by the Dhamma, and looking after one's relatives,
anavajjāni kammāni: etaṃ maṅgala-muttamaṃ.
(performing) actions that are blameless: this is the supreme blessing.

Ārati virati pāpā, majjapānā ca saññamo,
Abstinence, avoidance of bad deeds, restraint from intoxicating drink,
appamādo ca dhammesu: etaṃ maṅgala-muttamaṃ.
being heedful regarding (all) things: this is the supreme blessing.

Gāravo ca nivāto ca, santuṭṭhī ca kataññutā,
Having respect, being humble, being satisfied and grateful,
kālena dhamma-savaṇaṃ: etaṃ maṅgala-muttamaṃ.
listening to Dhamma at the right time: this is the supreme blessing.

Khantī ca sovacassatā, samaṇānañ-ca dassanaṃ,
Being patient and easily spoken to, seeing ascetics,
kālena dhamma-sākacchā: etaṃ maṅgala-muttamaṃ.
discussing Dhamma at the right time: this is the supreme blessing.

Tapo ca brahma-cariyañ-ca, ariya-saccāna-dassanaṃ,
Austere, living spiritually, insight into the noble truths,
nibbāna-sacchikiriyā ca: etaṃ maṅgala-muttamaṃ.
the experience of Nibbāna: this is the supreme blessing.

Phuṭṭhassa loka-dhammehi, cittaṃ yassa na kampati,
He whose mind does not waver, when it is touched by things of this world,
asokaṃ virajaṃ khemaṃ: etaṃ maṅgala-muttamaṃ.
(being) griefless, dustless, and secure: this is the supreme blessing.

Etādisāni katvāna, sabbattha-maparājitā,
Having done as here directed, they are undefeated everywhere,
sabbattha sotthiṃ gacchanti taṃ - tesaṃ maṅgala-muttaman"-ti.
they go everywhere in safety: for them this is the supreme blessing."

16. RATANA SUTTAṂ
DISCOURSE ON THE GEMS

Yānīdha bhūtāni samāgatāni, bhummāni vā yāni va antalikkhe,
Whatever beings have come together here, whether of the earth or in the firmament,
sabbe va bhūtā sumanā bhavantu, atho pi sakkacca suṇantu bhāsitaṃ.
may the minds of all those beings be happy, and may they listen carefully to what is said.
Tasmā hi bhūtā nisāmetha sabbe, mettaṃ karotha mānusiyā pajāya,
Therefore, all of you beings, be attentive, be friendly towards this generation of men,
divā ca ratto ca haranti ye baliṃ, tasmā hi ne rakkhatha appamattā.
they who bring offerings by day and by night, therefore, being heedful, you must protect them.

Yaṃ kiñci vittaṃ - idha vā huraṃ vā, saggesu vā - yaṃ ratanaṃ paṇītaṃ
Whatever riches there are - here or elsewhere or in the heavens - whatever excellent gem
na no samaṃ atthi tathāgatena, idam-pi buddhe ratanaṃ paṇītaṃ:
is not equal unto the Tathāgata, this excellent gem is in the Buddha:
etena saccena suvatthi hotu!
by virtue of this truth may there be safety!

Khayaṃ virāgaṃ amataṃ paṇītaṃ, yadajjhagā sakyamunī samāhito,
(Pollutants’) end, dispassion, deathlessness, excellence: which the Sākyan sage who is collected, attained ,
na tena dhammena samatthi kiñci, idam-pi dhamme ratanaṃ paṇītaṃ:
there is nothing that is equal to that *Dhamma*, this excellent gem is in the *Dhamma*:
etena saccena suvatthi hotu!
by virtue of this truth may there be safety!

Yaṃ-buddha seṭṭho parivaṇṇayī suciṃ, samādhi-mānantari-kañña-māhu,
That which the Buddha, the Great One, praised as pure, the *samādhi* said to have prompt (result),
samādhinā tena samo na vijjati, idam-pi dhamme ratanaṃ paṇītaṃ:
no equal to that *samādhi* is found, this excellent gem is in the Dhamma:
etena saccena suvatthi hotu!
by virtue of this truth may there be safety!

Ye puggalā aṭṭha sataṃ pasatthā, cattāri etāni yugāni honti,
Those eight individuals praised by the good, there are these four pairs (of individuals),
te dakkhiṇeyyā sugatassa sāvakā, etesu dinnāni mahapphalāni, idam-pi saṅghe ratanaṃ paṇītaṃ:
those disciples of the Sugata are worthy of gifts, those things that have been given to them have great fruit, this excellent gem is in the Saṅgha:
etena saccena suvatthi hotu!
by virtue of this truth may there be safety!

Ye suppa-yuttā manasā daḷhena, nikkāmino gotama-sāsanamhi,
Those who have firm and devoted minds, without sense desire in Gotama's dispensation,
te patti-pattā amataṃ vigayha, laddhā mudhā nibbutiṃ bhuñja-mānā,
those who have attained, and entered the deathless, are enjoying emancipation, gained for free,
idam-pi saṅghe ratanaṃ paṇītaṃ:
this excellent gem is in the Saṅgha:
etena saccena suvatthi hotu!
by virtue of this truth may there be safety!

Yathinda-khīlo paṭhaviṃ sito siyā, catubbhi vātehi asampa-kampiyo,
Just as a locking post stuck fast in the earth does not waver on account of the four winds,
tathūpamaṃ sappurisaṃ vadāmi, yo ariya saccāni avecca passati,
in the same way, I say, is the true person, the one who sees the noble truths completely,
idam-pi saṅghe ratanaṃ paṇītaṃ: etena saccena suvatthi hotu!
this excellent gem is in the Saṅgha: by virtue of this truth may there be safety!

Ye ariya-saccāni vibhāvayanti, gambhīra-paññena sudesitāni,
Those who clearly distinguish the noble truths, which were well preached by the one with deep wisdom,
kiñcāpi te honti bhusappa-mattā, na te bhavaṃ aṭṭhamaṃ ādiyanti,
however great they become in heedlessness still they do not take up an eighth existence,
idam-pi saṅghe ratanaṃ paṇītaṃ: etena saccena suvatthi hotu!
this excellent gem is in the Saṅgha: by virtue of this truth may there be safety!

Sahāvassa dassana-sampadāya, tayassu dhammā jahitā bhavanti:
With his attainment of (liberating) insight there are a triad of things that are given up:
sakkāya-diṭṭhi vicikicchitañ-ca, sīlabbataṃ vāpi yad-atthi kiñci.
embodiment view, uncertainty, and whatever (grasping at) virtue and practices there is.
Catūhapāyehi ca vippamutto, cha cābhi-ṭhānāni abhabbo kātuṃ,
He is free from (rebirth in) the four lower worlds, he is incapable of the six great crimes.
idam-pi Saṅghe ratanaṃ paṇītaṃ:
this excellent gem is in the Saṅgha:
etena saccena suvatthi hotu!
by virtue of this truth may there be safety!

Kiñcāpi so kammaṃ karoti pāpakaṃ, kāyena vācā uda cetasā vā,
Whatever bad action there is that he performs by way of body, or of speech, or of mind,
abhabbo so tassa paṭicchādāya, abhabbatā diṭṭha-padassa vuttā,
he is incapable of covering it up, this incapacity is said of one who has seen the state (of peace),
idam-pi saṅghe ratanaṃ paṇītaṃ: etena saccena suvatthi hotu!
this excellent gem is in the Saṅgha: by virtue of this truth may there be safety!

Vanappa-gumbe yathā phussi-tagge gimhāna-māse paṭhamasmiṃ gimhe,
Just like a tall woodland tree crowned with blossoms in the early summer months,
tathūpamaṃ dhamma-varaṃ adesayī, nibbāna-gāmiṃ paramaṃ-hitāya,
in the same way he preached the Dhamma which is best, which leads to Nibbāna, the highest benefit,
idam-pi buddhe ratanaṃ paṇītaṃ: etena saccena suvatthi hotu!
this excellent gem is in the Buddha: by virtue of this truth may there be safety!

Varo varaññū varado varāharo, anuttaro dhamma-varaṃ adesayī.

The noble one, knowing the noble state, giving the noble state, brought the noble state, unsurpassed, he preached the noble Dhamma.

idam-pi buddhe ratanaṃ paṇītaṃ: etena saccena suvatthi hotu!

this excellent gem is in the Buddha: by virtue of this truth may there be safety!

Khīṇaṃ purāṇaṃ navaṃ natthi sambhavaṃ, viratta-cittā āyatike bhavasmiṃ,

The old is destroyed, and nothing new is produced, (their) minds are unexcited by future rebirth,

te khīṇa-bījā avirūḷhi-cchandā, nibbanti dhīrā yathāyam-padīpo,

they have destroyed the seeds, and have no desire for growth, the wise are still, just as this lamp,

idam-pi saṅghe ratanaṃ paṇītaṃ: etena saccena suvatthi hotu!

this excellent gem is in the Saṅgha: by virtue of this truth may there be safety!

(Spoken by Sakka, lord of the gods:)

Yānīdha bhūtāni samāgatāni, bhummāni vā yāni va antalikkhe,

Whatever beings have come together here, whether of the earth or in the firmament,

tathāgataṃ deva-manussa-pūjitaṃ, buddhaṃ namassāma suvatthi hotu!

the Tathāgata is revered by gods and men, we honour the Buddha - may there be safety!

Yānīdha bhūtāni samāgatāni, bhummāni vā yāni va antalikkhe,

Whatever beings have come together here, whether of the earth or in the firmament,

tathāgataṃ deva-manussa-pūjitaṃ, dhammaṃ namassāma suvatthi hotu!

the Tathāgata is revered by gods and men, we honour the Dhamma - may there be safety!

Yānīdha bhūtāni samāgatāni, bhummāni vā yāni va antalikkhe,

Whatever beings have come together here, whether of the earth or in the firmament,

tathāgataṃ deva-manussa-pūjitaṃ, saṅghaṃ namassāma suvatthi hotu!

the Tathāgata is revered by gods and men, we honour the Saṅgha - may there be safety!

17. KARAṆĪYA-METTA SUTTAṂ
DISCOURSE ON LOVING KINDNESS PRACTICE.

Karaṇīya-mattha-kusalena, yaṃ taṃ santaṃ padaṃ abhi-samecca:

This is what should be done by one skilled in goodness, who understands the true path of peace:

sakko ujū ca sūjū ca, suvaco cassa mudu anatimānī,

They ought to be able and upright, straightforward, meek, and gentle in speech, humble and not conceited,

santussako ca subharo ca, appakicco ca sal-lahuka-vutti,

satisfied with little, easy to support, having little duties, frugal and light in living,

santindriyo ca nipako ca, appa-gabbho kulesu ana-nugiddho,

peaceful and calm , wise and skilful, not proud and detached from families

na ca khuddaṃ samācare kiñci, yena viññū pare upa-vadeyyuṃ.

They should not do the slightest thing that others, who are wise, might find fault in later on.

sukhino vā khemino hontu, sabbe sattā bhavantu sukhitattā!

(May all beings) be happy and secure! May all beings in their hearts be happy!

ye keci pāṇa-bhūtatthi, tasā vā thāvarā vā anavasesā,
Whatsoever living beings there are, weak or strong, omitting none,
dīghā vā ye mahantā vā, majjhimā rassa-kāṇuka-thūlā,
whether they be long or big bodied, medium, short or very small,
diṭṭhā vā ye va addiṭṭhā, ye ca dūre vasanti avidūre,
those who are seen, and those who are unseen, those who live far away, and those who are near,
bhūtā vā sambhavesī vā, sabbe sattā bhavantu sukhitattā!
those who are born, and those to be reborn, may all beings in their hearts be happy.

Na paro paraṃ nikubbetha, nātimaññetha katthaci naṃ kañci,
Let us not deceive one another, not despise anyone wherever he is.
byārosanā paṭigha-saññā, nāñña-maññassa dukkha-miccheyya.
Let us not wish another suffering by our anger or ill-will nor wish harm in any way.
mātā yathā niyaṃ puttaṃ, āyusā ekaputta-manurakkhe,
Even as a mother protects her only child by giving her life.

evam-pi sabba-bhūtesu, mānasaṃ bhāvaye apari-mānaṃ.
so too towards all living beings, mind should be developed endlessly.
Mettañ-ca sabba-lokasmiṃ, mānasaṃ bhāvaye aparimāṇaṃ,
radiating a mind of Loving Kindness over the entire world endlessly:
uddhaṃ adho ca tiriyañ-ca, asambādhaṃ averaṃ asapattaṃ.
above, below, and across (the middle), without barriers, hate, or hostility,
tiṭṭhaṃ caraṃ nisinno vā, sayāno vā yāvatassa vigata-middho,
whether standing, walking, sitting, or lying down as long as they are without drowsiness,
etaṃ satiṃ adhiṭṭheyya, brahmam-etaṃ vihāraṃ idhamāhu.
they should continue this recollection for this is said to be a sublime abiding.
Diṭṭhiñ-ca anupa-gamma sīlavā, dassanena sampanno,
By not holding onto fixed views, virtuous, with a harmonious perspective,
kāmesu vineyya gedhaṃ, na hi jātu gabbha seyyaṃ punaretī ti.
being freed from all sense desires, is not born again into this world.

18. KHANDHA PARITTAṂ (An Extraction)
THE SAFEGUARD OF THE CONSTITUENT GROUPS

Apādakehi me mettaṃ, mettaṃ dvipādakehi me,
I am friendly with those without feet, with those with two feet I am friendly,

catuppadehi me mettaṃ, mettaṃ bahuppadehi me.
I am friendly with those with four feet, with those with many feet I am friendly.

Mā maṃ apādako hiṃsi, mā maṃ hiṃsi dvipādako,
May the one without feet not hurt me, may the one with two feet not hurt me,

mā maṃ catuppado hiṃsi, mā maṃ hiṃsi bahuppado.
may the one with four feet not hurt me, may the one with many feet not hurt me.

Sabbe sattā, sabbe pāṇā, sabbe bhūtā ca kevalā,
May all beings, all living creatures, all who are born, in their entirety,

sabbe bhadrāni passantu, mā kañci pāpam-āgamā.
may all see prosperity, may nothing bad come to anyone

19. PUÑÑĀNU-MODANĀ
TRANSFERING MERITS

Dukkha-ppattā ca, niddukkhā
May suffering ones, be suffering free
Bhaya-ppattā ca, nibbhayā
And the fear-struck, fearless be
Sokappattā ca, nissokā
May the grieving, shed all grief
Hontu sabbe pi, pāṇino
And may all beings find relief.
Idaṃ no puññaṃ, sabbe sattā anumodantu
May all beings share this merit that we have thus acquired
sabba sampatti siddhiyā
For the acquisition of all kinds of happiness.
Ākāsaṭṭhā ca bhummaṭṭhā
May beings inhabiting space and earth
Devā nāgā mahiddhikā
Devas and nāgas of mighty power
Puññaṃ taṃ anumoditvā
Share this merit of ours.
Ciraṃ rakkhantu
May they long protect the
Buddhassa sāsanaṃ
Lord Buddha's dispensation.

Sādhu ... Sādhu... Sādhu

20. ĀSĪVĀDA
BLESSINGS

Sabbhītiyo vivajjantu — Sabba rogo vinassatu

May all misfortunes be averted, may all sickness be healed.

Mā te bhavat-vantarāyo — Sukhī dīghāyu kho bhava.

May no danger befall you, may you live long and happily.

Bhavatu sabba maṅgalaṃ — Rakkhantu sabba devatā

May all blessings be with you, may all *devas* protect you;

Sabba Buddhānu-bhāvena — Sadā sotthi bhavantu te.

By the power of all the Buddhas, may you be well and happy.

Bhavatu sabba maṅgalaṃ — Rakkhantu sabba devatā

May all blessings be with you, may all devas protect you;

Sabba dhammānu-bhāvena — Sadā sotthi bhavantu te.

By the power of all the Dhamma, may you be well and happy.

Bhavatu sabba maṅgalaṃ — Rakkhantu sabba devatā

May all blessings be with you, may all devas protect you;

Sabba saṅghānu-bhāvena — Sadā sotthi bhavantu te.

By the power of all the Saṅgha, may you be well and happy.

Abhivādana, sīlissa

For one who habitually shows respect,

niccaṁ vaddhā-pacāyino

constantly respectful of elders,

cattāro dhammā vaḍḍhanti

four states increase:

āyu vaṇṇo sukhaṁ balaṃ

age, beauty, happiness and strength.

A GUIDE TO PRONUNCIATION OF PĀLI

Pāli is the beautiful language of the early Buddhist scriptures. It is based on an Indian dialect that was spoken in the area where the Buddha did most of his teaching, and therefore must be very close to the language that the Buddha used during his 45 years of teaching. Without any doubt the Theravāda scriptures, which are preserved in the Pāḷi language contain the most faithful record of what the Buddha actually taught, so for those who are earnestly striving to put the Buddha's teaching into practice it is a great advantage to be able to read and understand the language of the text.

Pāḷi is notable for both its fluency and its rhythm, and there is no easier or quicker way to become acquainted with the language than through reciting the texts aloud, which will soon familiarize the student with key words and phrases which recur in the text, and at the same time will give a feel for the structure of the language. Below is an introduction to the pronunciation of Pāḷi, together with some notes to help clarify some of the difficulties that are encountered by those unfamiliar with Indian languages.

The Alphabet:

Vowels:	a	ā	i	ī	u	ū	e	o
Pure nasal:	ṃ							
Consonants:	ka	kha	ga	gha	ṅa			
	ca	cha	ja	jha	ña			
	ṭa	ṭha	ḍa	ḍha	ṇa			
	ta	tha	da	dha	na			
	pa	pha	ba	bha	ma			
Semi vowels, sibilant, and aspirate:	ya	ra	la	ḷa	va	sa	ha	

This is the basic pattern of all the Indian alphabets, and as can be seen, they are arranged on a very rational basis. First come the vowels (discussed below), followed by the pure nasal. Next come the definite consonants with their corresponding nasal sounds. These are organised according to their place of articulation, beginning with the gutturals pronounced at the back of the mouth, and ending with those articulated on the lips. Then come the indefinite consonants. There are five main difficulties for those unfamiliar with the Indian languages, which will be dealt with here.

Unlike English, for instance, the vowel system in Pāḷi is very precise, and the vowels are either short or long, with the latter being exactly twice as long as the former. It is important to distinguish the lengths of the vowels correctly, as a, for example, is a negative prefix; but *ā* is an intensifier (*ananda* means unhappy; *ānanda* means very happy). As a guide for the English reader:

A	as in another
Ā	as in art
I	as in ink
Ī	as in eel
U	as in manure
Ū	as in prudent
E	as in age (but before a conjunct consonant as in end)
O	as in own (but before a conjunct consonant as in orange)

Only one letter is used to represent the sounds *e* & *o*, which are normally pronounced long as *ē*, & *ō*. Before a conjunct they are normally pronounced short as *ĕ*, & *ŏ*, although it appears to be the case that when these vowels appear in *sandhi* before a double consonant, they retain their natural length, and should be pronounced as such, so that in *jarādhammo 'mhi*, we should read *jarādhammō 'mhi*.

The second and fourth letters in the consonant section of the alphabet (*kha gha cha jha* etc.), are digraphs representing the aspirate sound of the preceding consonant (*ka ga ca ja* etc.). They are pronounced as the latter, but with a strong breath pulse. Again, these must be distinguished (*kamati*, for example, is not *khamati*). Note that simple *ca* is pronounced as in change, cha is the same with a stronger breath pulse.

In Pāḷi *ṭa ṭha* ḍa & *ḍha* are pronounced with the tongue behind the dental ridge, giving a characteristic hollow sound. The sounds *ta tha* da & *dha* are pronounced with the tip of the tongue on the teeth. In English *ta* & *da* etc. are about halfway between the two, so move the tongue back for the first group, and forward for the second. Note that *tha* is never pronounced as in they or their, but is the aspirate of *ta*.

The nasal sounds are all distinguished according to their place of articulation. This in practice causes few problems when the nasal is in conjunction with one of its corresponding consonants. But some of them (*ña ṇa na* & *ma*) occur by themselves also, so again they must be recognised and pronounced according to their correct position. The sound of each can be found by pronouncing them before a member of their group, e.g. first *ṅ* as in ink. The pronunciation of *ña* is as in canyon, or the Spanish word *señore*. The letter ṃ represents the pure nasal which is sounded when the air escapes through the nose only.

Double consonants must be clearly articulated as two sounds, not merged into one, as is the tendency in European languages. When there is a double consonant it may help to imagine a hyphen between the two letters and pronounce accordingly. Therefore *sut-taṃ*, not *sutaṃ* (or *sūtaṃ*); *bhik-khu*, not *bhikhu* (or *bhīkhu*) etc.

To get a feel for the pronunciation and rhythm of the language it is strongly advised that beginners join in group chanting with people who are experienced in the language until they are able to manage the correct pronunciation by themselves. This will also help in familiarising students with certain basic texts.

Below is a guide to the correct pronunciation of the language, summarising the points discussed above, together with some further information regarding articulation.

a	is short as in another, academic		
ā	is long as in art, father		
i	is short as in ink, pin		
ī	is long as in eel, seal		
u	is short as in mature, manure		
ū	is long as in prudent, do		
e	is long in open syllables as in age, but before a conjunct consonant it is short as in end		
o	is long in open syllables as in own, but before a conjunct consonant it is short as in orange		
ṃ	is the pure nasal sounded through the nose like in thinking		
k	as in cat, keen	kh	somewhat as in black heath
g	as in gadfly, gate	gh	somewhat as in log house or ghost.

ṅ	as in bank		
c	as in change, church	ch	somewhat as in witch hazel
j	as in jet, jaw	jh	somewhat as in sledge hammer
ñ	as in canyon, señor		

The following sounds as noted but with the tongue drawn back, thereby producing a hollow sound:

ṭ	as in tap, tick	ṭh	somewhat as in ant hill (never as in they)
ḍ	as in did, dug	ḍh	somewhat as in red hot
ṇ	as in know		

The following sounds as noted but with the tongue touching the tip of the teeth:

t	as in tub, ten	th	somewhat as in cat house
d	as in den, dig	dh	somewhat as in mad house
n	as in nip, nose		

p	as in pat, pinch	ph	somewhat as in top hat (never as in photo)
b	as in back, big	bh	somewhat as in abhorrence
m	as in men, mice		
y	as in yes, year	r	as in red, but with a stronger trill
l	as in lead, lend	ḷ	as before, but with the tongue drawn back like in illusion
v	at the beginning of a word, as in van, vane, elsewhere it more closely resembles wan, wane		
s	as in say, send	h	as in hat, height

[Based On a guide prepared by Ānandajothi Bhikkhu at: http://www.buddhanet-de.net/ancient-buddhist-texts/Reference/The-Pronunciation-of-Pali.htm]
(some additional pronunciation words have been added by Bhante Kusala).

NOTES AND QUESTIONS:

34388988R00032

Printed in Great Britain
by Amazon